A Widow's Journey

A Widow's Journey

A Story of Love, Loss,
and
Letting Go

Gilda Zelin

iUniverse, Inc.
New York Bloomington Shanghai

A Widow's Journey
A Story of Love, Loss, and Letting Go

Copyright © 2008 by Gilda Zelin

iUniverse books may be ordered through booksellers or by contacting:

iUniverse
1663 Liberty Drive
Bloomington, IN 47403
www.iuniverse.com
1-800-Authors (1-800-288-4677)

Because of the dynamic nature of the Internet, any Web addresses or links contained in this book may have changed since publication and may no longer be valid.

The views expressed in this work are solely those of the author and do not necessarily reflect the views of the publisher, and the publisher hereby disclaims any responsibility for them.

Photographs courtesy of Gilda Zelin and Courtnay Perry

Cover Design: Courtnay Perry

ISBN: 978-0-595-46587-3 (pbk)
ISBN: 978-0-595-90883-7 (ebk)

Printed in the United States of America

This journey is dedicated to all my children:

Ken, Missy, Karen, Bill, Richard, and Debbie

To Gay,

Sincerely yours.

Gilda

Contents

Aptos California 1991

Preface

On August 25, 2005, Adonai, who resides in the upper ethereal world, in his most infinite wisdom, let out a bolt of lightning and my beloved husband of fifty-seven years, Joel Zelin, died of congestive heart failure. Joel's health had been failing for two years and I had been his primary caregiver.

When my husband died, I felt as if I had swallowed a knotted rope that stretched from my larynx down to my groin. My insides constricted and inflated. I couldn't eat, I lost weight, and I had to take an acid reducer to stop the voluminous belching. If not for my daughter (who became the mother), two recent widows, a single woman, and a telephone buddy who had the time to listen to me without criticism, I would have drowned in self-pity and loneliness.

I spent the blurred months after Joel's death trying to make sense of my new feelings about life and trying to understand the new sensations in my body. I was, in many ways, paralyzed. It wasn't until I fell under the tutelage of a writing teacher, seven months after my husband's death, that the knotted rope I'd swallowed began to work its way out of my system, each essay I wrote untying one more knot until I could finally breathe clearly. The act of writing enabled me to survive that excruciating first year.

My writing teacher prompted me to open my heart and mind and put my thoughts on paper. Not being a seasoned writer, I simply wrote as I felt the need to write: sometimes in the form of a letter to Joel, other times with a definite subject or stream of ideas flowing from my heart to the paper.

This book, the final product of that writing therapy, is a journal of my experiences and thoughts, not necessarily in chronological order, but documented as each idea or event came to mind when provoked by a memory or an incident from the past. I have used italics when speaking to Joel, to avoid confusion in reading.

I am now a seventy-eight years young widow, in good health. I loved deeply for fifty-seven years, traveled, and tasted the best of food and wine—but now I am single and no longer part of a couple. My lifelong partner has died.

While I have finally accepted the reality of this, it's still difficult, as an older single woman, to be back in the world. Am I just another fifth wheel who doesn't want to be put in the back bedroom or left out of a conversation because of age or lack of knowledge, or who causes an imbalance at a dinner table? Does a person have to be coupled in order to be accepted in our society? I know I'm not the only widow facing life from this new, uncomfortable perch, and I know many more before me have been in the same position. Still, the problem of finding a place for my new self is not easily resolved.

Many books have been written about grief and how survivors can cope with the death of a loved one. None have helped me, a woman who has loved deeply and lost a great friend, who has raised a wonderful family, who has lived well and now is left with a deep void.

That is why I have decided to share the very private affairs of my life. I now know that a woman who becomes a widow at seventy or eighty years of age *can* have a life, even though, to most of society, we are a forgotten group. I want other widows to profit from the difficult journey I began on the day my husband died. My experiences, and the conclusions I have reached, may give others the will and the ability to reach out to people and to continue living a full life, rather than becoming an "old lady," abandoned by family and society both.

Let me take you through my period of grief and mourning. Let me show you how I fought my way back into a world in which there seemed to be no place for a woman like me.

In the beginning there was darkness ...

"Gilda, I am fainting."

These were his last words. I had no time to answer as I raced into the bathroom. There were no hugs, not even an *I love you,* and so started my widow's journey.

The medics arrived, put him on a gurney, and left for the emergency room. They asked if I wanted to come with them. I said no. The adrenaline was racing at high speed through my body; my thinking was clear and precise.

It was 4:45 a.m. Thursday when I called and woke my son-in-law. My daughter was in the country with their two children, relishing the last days of summer vacation. "Bill," I said, "Joel just died. The paramedics are taking him to the hospital. I'll be there."

Methodically I turned off all the lights in the house, gathered my wallet and cell phone into my pocket, and looked around to make sure everything was secure. Alone, I followed the ambulance to the hospital. I didn't allow myself to think. I concentrated on the road. Carefully I parked, locked the door and walked briskly into the hospital. I didn't know who I was. High on adrenaline, I felt like another person inhabited my body. The key word here is *alone*—I didn't realize it at the time.

Two of the medics met me, and one put his arm around my shoulder and led me into a cubicle. There was Joel on a gurney, covered to the neck with a sheet. The medics encircled us with curtains and we were alone. I stood beside my beloved and reached for his hand under the cover. It was still very warm. I remember feeling numb as I patted his arm, smoothed his brow and held his hand. Still not comprehending reality, I spoke softly, telling him everything was going to be all right. I kissed his forehead and I felt the warmth leaving his body, just as the adrenaline rush was leaving mine. The colder he became, the number I became.

I don't know what I was thinking during those moments. It just seemed as if time was standing still and my husband and I were in a vacuum; there was no movement, no sound. I don't even know how long I stood in that emergency room cubicle.

Suddenly I became aware of the curtains parting and conversations going on behind me; my son-in-law and my grandson, who had a summer job working in Santa Cruz, had arrived. The three of us sat around Joel's body, not talking. In our life as a couple, I was not the crier. Joel, always very sentimental, was the one who cried easily. As I sat near his body, moaning and rocking back and forth, I began to berate him for leaving me so suddenly. I tried to maintain control, as I had done all my life, but feelings of rage broke through.

No one came to tell us what to do. We just sat in the cold gray cubicle, watching Joel as though we fully expected him to wake up. I sighed and moaned until the vigil was finally broken by my daughter's arrival from the country, followed shortly by the news that the funeral director would be taking Joel's body to the chapel as soon as the cause of death had been established and a death certificate issued by the county. Like an automaton, I reacted to gentle orders, prompted by the various arms at my elbow directing me from place to place.

Night was beginning to fall as we left the hospital. Joel's body had been removed to the funeral parlor. Medical and coroner papers had been signed and confirmed. We were free to go. Someone suggested we stop for coffee and maybe a sandwich. Where we ate or what we ate is beyond my recall; for me, it was simply a delaying tactic for the inevitable return home.

It took all my strength to make my feelings clear to my children. I did not need company this night. There was no reason for people to hover around me.

As soon as I locked the door behind them, I slipped to the floor, sobbing with remorse. As I sat there, trying to collect myself, the realization hit me: I am a widow. How does a widow act? How does a widow dress? Do I wear a big "W" when I go outside? Am I still me?

Finally in control, I stood up and braced myself on the walls to walk down the hall. Passing the bathroom where the final moments had occurred, I noticed that the medics had cleaned up pretty well; only the stains from my beloved's life fluids remained on the floor.

My weak legs carried me into our bedroom and I threw myself upon the empty, cold bed. Thankfully overpowered by both physical and mental exhaustion, I fell asleep.

The next day, my family and I went to the funeral parlor to make arrangements for the funeral. The solemnity of the funeral director, the delicacy in his explanation of what would occur, and the peculiar odor that infused my nostrils in those rooms are things I will always remember. How many chairs would I need, how many yarmulkes? How did I spell my husband's Hebrew name? Who will speak at the gravesite? I drifted off and looked at this man. What kind of person could possibly want a job like this, repeating the same speech daily with that soothing voice, trying to be kind and understanding, wanting to honor the every wish of the bereaved?

His voice droned on and on, apologizing along the way, but he had to have the information. I let my children deal with it. I really didn't care, because Joel was coming home from the hospital soon and I had no interest in all of this.

I should have seen the signs, when he sat in his blue chair and seemed to reflect within himself. For the last month or so, he would bring up stories of his youth, or when the children were young, or when we were young. Rather than talking about the present and future, he dwelled on the past. There was also the cramping that occurred in dialysis regularly, and the decrease of white blood cells that caused the Dialysis Center to include an antibiotic in the last fifteen minutes of the blood transfer. We began seeing more doctors to determine the problem, and he became more tranquil, not as opinionated as usual. There didn't seem to be any fighting back in his attitude.

Was there a moment in his day, as he sat in his chair, that he thought he was dying? Sometimes he looked at me bustling around with a strange expression on his face. Did he hate me for being the one who could wheel him around, run errands, carry loads of laundry or packages from the garage? Did he resent me, knowing that he was now incapable of sharing the basic household chores?

Joel, so intent was I, in the moments of these last few days, trying to help you emotionally through the spasms of wracking pain, that I did not have time to step back and see what was really occurring. If the doctors couldn't stop this process of dying, could I have at least delayed it?

I mentally listed his medical problems: bleeding—involuntary and spontaneous, internally and externally, failure to clot, low red blood cell count, diabetes, arthritis, gout, inability to feel the bottom of his feet, scoliosis of the spine, liquid retention, high blood pressure, high cholesterol, thyroid problems, body rash, congestive heart failure, irregular heartbeat, kidney dialysis.

There were so many operations available that would ease his way, but no surgeon would touch him, except in a life or death situation, because of his bleeding problem. When he had his heart attack, he was infused with blood platelets for three days until his red blood count was sufficient. Only when the doctors felt that waiting was a bigger risk than the bleeding problem did they replace the main artery in his heart. When I finally cleaned his bathroom medicine chest, I threw out fourteen different kinds of pain relievers and eighteen prescription medications.

The last two years of his life were hard on both of us. Thankfully, we were able to forge ahead as positively as possible, not least because Joel never lost his desire to be with me, nor did I ever waiver in my commitment to him.

Gilda and Joel Zelin 1948

To tell you who Joel was is to tell you who we were. At the age of twenty we were already a close-knit couple, unencumbered by a TV set, a cell phone, or a computer. There was a lightness to life then. We were free and we lived in the moment. It was a different time, a different generation; you might call it the age of innocence.

We met at a New York beach on the Fourth of July weekend in 1947, the only place a Bronx boy could meet a Brooklyn girl. We were nineteen.

We were married within a year because both sets of parents, European immigrants with strong Victorian morals, felt our relationship was getting too serious. As my mother said, wagging her finger at Joel, "Even though you are engaged, there are still no benefits until after the wedding." We listened, the fear and shame of getting pregnant before marrying uppermost in my mind.

It could almost be said that Joel and I were joined at the hip. We were lovers, husband and wife, and most of all best friends. We were happy too, although never introspective, never delving into our inner thoughts. As time passed, we continued to adapt to one another's needs. This was our secret; we were complete.

In his twenties, Joel was, as we called it, "establishing himself." Only one year out of his teens, he entered the family business, found that he enjoyed it, worked from 5:30 a.m. to 6:00 p.m. every weekday, and came home to what the current generation calls a "TV housewife." When he arrived home after his work day, my hair was combed, I was dressed and dinner was ready. When the children eventually arrived, they were usually bathed, fed and ready for bed. This was the routine of our mothers' houses. It is what we knew.

We were concerned about how we looked, about manners and about what our parents thought. This is what was expected of us, and we were happy. We didn't analyze our lives or long for anything different. In today's world, this might not seem possible, but it was the truth.

Joel had a voracious appetite. Before we were married, his mother invited me for dinner and I watched as she served him a whole chuck steak, which he finished. This was a forecast of things to come. Pasta was one of Joel's favorites, and every Thursday night during our marriage I'd make him a pound of pasta, topped lightly with an Italian sauce I had cooked for hours. This quickly became known as "Pasta for Joelie" night. If by some chance there were leftovers, he would eat them for breakfast. In those years, weight was not a problem for him.

Halloween party 1955

The author, age 16

When we bought our first house on borrowed money, Joel became the gardener, electrician and plumber. He was very good with his hands and could fix anything. To save money, we did not go out very often. Instead, we socialized with our neighbors on the block. Joel rigged up a system that would alert us if one of our children needed help while we were visiting other homes.

We were at a party one evening and someone asked Joel if he had the "seven-year itch," since he'd married at such a young age. He put his arm around my shoulder and answered that anything he ever needed, he found at home. As he closed out his twenties, Joel was paying off a mortgage, paying back money he borrowed to get the mortgage, and was the father of three children.

In his thirties, Joel learned how to better manage the stress caused by work, and how to be a more focused father and husband at home. Was life a bed of roses? Of course not. There were business crises to deal with, teenage catastrophes to handle and major financial breakdowns that sent our budget into dizzying collapse, but we learned how to adjust and readjust our lives together. This was a real growing-up period for Joel, a compromising period. Flexibility was the key word. He learned to juggle the everyday events of business and family using integrity and honesty, building a strong foundation in his character that he passed on to his family.

We became a fishing family when Joel bought a twenty-foot cabin cruiser that we named the "5 Zs." Crabbing and fluke fishing in the Atlantic Ocean kept us well fed and together for many weekends. Joel had season tickets to Jets and Giants football games and he managed Little League teams. All of these activities were family inclusive, never a chore, simply fun events that occupied our weekends and summer nights. Winning and losing were not on our minds; it was togetherness that counted.

Joel began to reap the benefits of his hard work and family during his forties. We went to the theater constantly and ate in better restaurants. He started to develop a taste for good food that didn't depend on quantity. He also had more time to enjoy his children though they were scattered throughout the country, living first in college dormitories, and then with spouses. Wherever they were, the Sunday morning telephone call from him was a regular event. He was the "big Daddy"—larger than life, involved in everyone and everything that surrounded him. There were many proud moments in Joel's life, but one that stands out is when he became a grandfather for the first time. We called all of our friends, and even though there was a big snowstorm raging in New York that day, they all came over and we had an instant party.

Hawaii 1991

North Shore Long Island 1962

As we approached our 50s, *Europe on $5 a Day* by Arthur Frommer became our Bible. We followed it religiously throughout Italy, France and England. Each summer we chose another area to explore. During these trips Joel developed a love for wine as well as an understanding of the grape, its various growing climates, and the times to plant and harvest. He realized that wine had a living personality and that once a year's growth was gone, there would never be another like it. Needless to say, his love for different types of cooking grew during these times as well.

Whatever Joel did, he did with a passion. He also had a mind like a steel trap. Through years of reading and traveling he accumulated bits of what he called "useless information" and was able to discuss almost any topic with some knowledgeable authority. When we began to take cruises he was a killer in the trivia contests we entered, and we had a drawer full of key chain and luggage tag prizes to prove it.

If Joel had been maturing during his twenties and thirties, in his sixties he really ripened. He was then able to harvest and enjoy the life that he had established earlier through trial and error. His humor, knowledge and willingness to share made him welcome everywhere. I was right by his side, sharing every experience. We were a twosome.

When Joel retired, we left New York for a new home in California. Joel joined a temple immediately, quickly becoming active in the various programs that were available. Temples always played an important role in our lives. In our extensive travels, we always sought out temples and left donations. Joel became president of our Temple the same year that our son in Ohio became president of his. We joked about our family's power across the country.

It was through our new California Temple that Joel found his true calling in community theater. He produced shows and even appeared in one of the Temple plays as a rabbi who is murdered in the first act. His quick wit enabled him to emcee Temple events and he was at his best onstage, in front of an audience, telling jokes and introducing speakers or acts. The little boy from the Bronx had come a long way and he was enjoying every minute of it.

As Joel entered his seventies, he reveled in his growing family, and he was still traveling and enjoying his wine and food. We were financially stable and our lives were rich and full of good experiences. But in the way that life often gives with one hand and takes with another, this period also marked the beginning of Joel's health problems. Different parts of his body started to break down, each part wanting more and more, until finally they all erupted and there was darkness in my life.

In retrospect, one always tends to glorify a loved one. I am fully aware that there were many faults in Joel's character. He was human, and capable of anger, jealousy and resentment just like everyone else. I realize, however, that while trying to capture the essence of my beloved in an overview, I have written a eulogy instead.

⋘⊙⋙

Monday, August 2nd
You had terrible pain in your body. We raced to the E.R. The pain was so intense that your eyes were popping out of your head. They gave you a shot of morphine and you were relieved immediately. We went home because you refused to be admitted to the hospital.

<u>*Tuesday, August 23rd*</u>
We went to see the doctor and he could not find anything that would cause such debilitating pain throughout your body.

<u>*Wednesday, August 24th*</u>
The torturous pain returned and we went back to the doctor. He gave you two prescriptions, one a liquid and one a pill. You took both when we got home. You had no appetite for dinner. You took your medication and we went to sleep.

<u>*Thursday, August 25th, 3:50 am*</u>
"Gilda, take me to the E.R. I cannot urinate."
"Gilda, I am fainting."

<u>*Thursday, August 25th, 4:15 am*</u>
The End.

⌖

    While I am not a very religious person (by that I mean going to services regularly), it is my sincere belief that religious rites kept me grounded and gave me a feeling of security when my life was thrown into chaos. I was overwhelmed with new responsibilities—paying bills, finding legal papers, dealing with lawyers, accountants and the I.R.S., all while grieving for the man I loved. Religious rituals gave me a time zone, a structured framework that made me focus and helped to stabilize the havoc in my life. No matter how incompetent, insecure or dazed I felt, the various observances gave me a raison d'etre for the first year. After each religious ceremony I experienced a deeper connection to Joel.

Thousands of years have passed since these rituals first became practice, but they still serve us. We are still human beings, searching for the meaning of life, with the same emotions, desires and need for stability. These rituals establish order from chaos. They help the bereaved accept and find comfort in the life and death passages of their lives.

There exists in my Temple a group of sainted people called the *Chevra Kaddisha* who perform the ritual service of bathing the deceased before burial. This has been the Jewish tradition for nearly fifty-eight hundred years. After Joel's death, my daughter and I both wanted to be present at this ceremony.

The next day, Friday, we were ushered into a cold, damp, high-ceilinged room with huge slop sinks and long silver extension hoses. The body of my husband lay on a metal bed. His head rested on a block and he was covered in a white sheet. A neon light hovered low from the high ceiling.

My daughter and I were placed on the outside perimeter of the room. Four women and two men busily filled pails with water from the sink. They walked over to the body. Two women took their places on one side of the body near the head and torso, the other two stood directly opposite them on the other side. The two men stood on either side of Joel's body between his torso and his toes. The Rabbi stood at the head of the body chanting prayers for the dead.

The ancient ritual began, and it almost felt as though I were watching a ballet in slow motion. First the head was bathed on either side with tenderness and care. Each arm was raised and bathed, held as if it were a delicate flower, then the torso. Each woman moved around the body as if in a dance, paying homage, then they all stopped. The sensitivity of the next part was unbearable. The women averted their eyes while the men washed his private parts and feet, thus honoring this body as a person, a man whom they knew when he was very much alive. Delicately and sympathetically, they preserved his modesty, all this in silent reverence.

They transferred his body to a clean trolley lined with white cotton gauze. First they wrapped the head, then the body. They put his *tallit* (prayer shawl) around his shoulders and his *tefillin* (phylacteries) in his hands with devout care and kindness. Something happened to me in that room as I sat watching. I realized that the bond between two people who grew up together and lived together for fifty-seven years cannot be broken.

There is an episode of "Seinfeld" that Joel and I saw together, in which Jerry and Kramer are up in the gallery watching an operation. Down below, doctors and nurses huddle over the patient. Kramer begins to hiss "Psst, psst!" louder and louder, until all the doctors look up. "Move over!" he shouts. "I can't see!" For a while when they were washing Joel's body, they were clustered around him in such a way that I couldn't see. I found myself smiling. If I could have seen his face, I know he would have been smiling too. This was one of those times when two people know from a nod, a look, a smile, a squeeze of a hand, what the other is thinking. This is our bond. It is eternal.

When they finished their wrapping and stepped back from the table, my beloved was gone. Only a mummy-like figure remained. The casket was rolled in, and for a fleeting moment I wondered how they would lift this figure up and into it. Besides being cumbersome, I knew how heavy Joel was. Then I worried whether the casket was long enough for this wrapped body. In thinking about these logistics, I realized that I was disassociating myself from this body. I began gasping for breath at my guilty thoughts. This was not an object. This was my beloved. I must have had an anxiety attack, because when I came back to the moment, I found that the six people had lifted Joel's bathed and swathed figure into his final resting place, the coffin. Someone was gently asking if I wanted to help roll it into the funeral chapel. I nodded, and slowly we guided the casket in.

The physical remains of my beloved were gone forever. But in some way, I felt a little closure. My sweetie was treated with love and dignity. We were close through a lifetime of memories, and that closeness remained, even in death.

All day Saturday people came to pay their respects. That is when the real numbness set in, and it lasted for several weeks. I was like a robot, moving when people told me to move, sitting when I was told, eating when someone placed food before me.

Another Jewish tradition that proved very meaningful for me involves sitting with a body until it is interred. A group of devoted people stay with the body, quietly praying and protecting it, and if necessary consoling anyone in need. There was always someone there to sit with Joel, all through Friday and Saturday, day and night, until he was wheeled out on Sunday, put into the hearse, and driven to the cemetery.

The sitters provided me with the opportunity to go home to try and rest. At home, my family kept talking and prodding me with food. I know it was all in my best interests, but I just wanted to be alone, to have a quiet time by myself.

On that Sunday, I was not at the funeral parlor when it was time to take my beloved to his final resting place. He was waiting for me at the cemetery.

◦◦◦

Thoughts of the funeral day stream into my mind frequently, even after nine months of widowhood. In my younger days I could have produced a new life in this time. Today I can only produce memories of a funeral and the finality of the interment.

I don't remember many of the details of this early morning. I do remember thinking about a tradition in India that requires the wife to throw herself on the funeral pyre of her husband because there is no life for her once he is gone.

I don't remember how I dressed that day or what I had for breakfast. I don't remember riding in a car with my family to the cemetery, how I got there, where we met, whose car we were in.

I do remember standing outside the gates to the cemetery and nodding to the multitudes that passed by, people from all phases of Joel's life: people from the coffee shop, merchants, businessmen, relatives we don't speak to; people from restaurants, friends, the neighborhood. It was endless.

I do remember not being able to stand anymore. Someone walked me to the gravesite and I sat down in front of a huge hole with a mound of dirt on one side.

I remember the woeful wail of Dan Phillips' clarinet playing softly from afar. Sitting there in my solitude, I don't remember if the sun was shining, if I was hot or cold, if my mind was clear or a blur of memories. I remember the constant flow of tears that blurred my vision.

I do remember looking up and seeing an endearing sight that would have made Joel very proud. Trudging down the path to the grave were six wonderful men, sons, son-in-law, grandsons, carrying his casket to its final resting place. So endearing yet so heartbreaking, grappling with the clumsiness of their burden until they had it nestled safely in the earth.

There were prayers by the Rabbi, heartfelt thoughts spoken by many. Others came up to the podium and tried to speak, but did not succeed. They were too overwhelmed with emotion. In the background, I heard crying and sobbing at the words being spoken. What they were and who was speaking, I cannot remember.

I do remember being helped to my feet and given the first shovel full of dirt to throw on the casket, and each person doing the same in tribute to Joel.

I don't remember when the Rabbi pinned the traditional torn black ribbon on my jacket to remind me and my family of our loss. This ribbon was worn all during the Shiva period, the seven days of mourning observed after a Jewish funeral.

I don't know how I left the funeral grounds or how I got home. I remember a crowd of people in the house. I know I took a lot of deep breaths as I moved among them, trying not to arouse their sympathy for fear I would break down. Eventually they all went home and I was left with my children. When my children left, it was only me, alone on my husband's funeral day—August 28, 2005.

During the Shiva week, in some way food arrived every day to feed our family. I don't remember what I did during the days. It was a blur. People came in and out of the house, some bearing food, some condolences. Many people arrived in the evening for *Yahrzeit* (prayers for the dead) services. The week, filled with people, food preparation, and a constant whirl of activity, slipped by.

When it ended, my new life began. I looked ahead, keeping in mind the words of some very wise writers in a Yiddish folk song, and hoping that the people in my world would under-stand me and the depth of my loss, and be kind.

Weep before G-d and laugh before people.

—Yiddish folk song

Eight months into widowhood, as I attended a Passover Seder in the social hall of the Temple, surrounded by friends and a multitude of other people, I thought back to one year ago when my sweetie and I were sharing the same experience. Since then, the angel of death decided not to pass over our house. He came and my darling surrendered to him. Even though I used all my strength and will to keep him alive, I lost the battle.

My mind wandered and I returned to that night, remembering his frantic call, "Gilda, you have to take me to the E.R., I cannot urinate." It was 3:50 a.m. as I dragged myself out of bed, accustomed to this routine. One more time we would go to the emergency room. The anonymous faces would listen to our story, trying to look concerned but just doing their jobs. They would list all his symptoms, patch him up as best they could, and we would drive home, just another incident among many in our lives.

I had dressed as quickly as I could on that morning, suggesting he go to the bathroom while he waited for me. And for some reason, though I rarely used it and it was almost always turned off or uncharged, I put the cell phone into my pocket immediately. Suddenly I heard him cry out, "Gilda, I am fainting." I rushed into the bathroom and encircled him in my arms, trying to keep him from falling to the floor. I kept talking to him, urging him to help me. I could not sustain his weight. He smiled at me, relaxed, and slipped out of my arms to the cold floor. I knew what had happened, but would not admit to myself that the greatest tragedy of my life had just occurred. Holding his head, I called 9-1-1.

Sometimes I think that in every tragedy there exists bizarre comedy. There I was, struggling to keep him alive on the toilet seat. The picture of this, while I wandered outside my body to view the scene, made me smile. With my will and strength I thought I could bring him back again as we had done so many times before, and the two of us would laugh about what happened in the bathroom. The picture of me, a hundred pounds lighter than he, straddling his body on the toilet seat, would certainly keep us laughing as we repeated the scene when it was over and all was fine again.

The wail of the ambulance and the incessant clang of the fire truck finally stopped in front of our house. Gently I put his head back on the floor and opened the door. Six men and women marched into action. I walked out of the bathroom. One finally asked me if they should keep trying to revive him. I nodded as they carted him off to the hospital on a gurney. I followed him in my car. I knew, but with all my body and soul I didn't want to know. He died in my arms, but we never had the time to say *I love you*. All these thoughts meandered through my mind as I brought myself back to reality and to the present Passover story. We needed more time together. Why must this year be different from all other years?

As time passes, I realize that my deep emotions are no longer visible. The heavy sobbing has stopped. The tears that gathered and flowed constantly have stopped. Both have passed inward. And yet, when I bumped into two acquaintances recently, both wanting to know where Joel was as they looked for him over my shoulder, the tears swarmed out.

Inward, outward, all contradictions—but *over* was the truth. The angel of death did not pass over.

When I look back to the months after Joel died, I can't remember all of the emotions I experienced. I do remember keeping myself busy, too busy, running, running, running, and trying not to think about my present life.

I spent each frantic day leaving my empty house at 10 a.m. and trying not to return until 5 or 6 p.m. If I refer to my calendar, I can see that each day was power-packed with things to do. I don't remember if I did these things effectively or not. I don't remember if I paid all the bills, took care of the laundry, or took the garbage out on time. Obviously I did, as no threatening letters have arrived from collection agencies. I assume I followed my life patterns by rote.

My mind is so cluttered with memories that sometimes I don't remember why I entered a room or what it is I am looking for. I don't remember—or is it that I don't want to remember?

⋘⋙

After the Shiva period my mailbox was flooded with more than two hundred condolence cards. The ones that comforted me the most were the handwritten notes. It was impossible to thank every person who wrote, so I resolved this by placing an ad in the Temple's monthly publication, thanking people for their kind remembrances. I knew that not everyone who sent a card would see that ad, but they would have to understand that social graces were far from my mind at that time.

The avalanche of relentless daily mail and the urgency of making day-to-day decisions while feeling so emotionless and fatigued drove me to distraction. Even trying to accomplish the simplest tasks caused great frustration. One of the biggest culprits was automated phone systems, and the inability to speak with a live person without responding to a long, tangled list of electronic commands.

I was able to vent some of my despair and anger through writing, but writing did not ease my loneliness or feelings of abandonment.

My lifestyle changed—I was suddenly able to leave the house for hours, engage in physical activities and join women's groups. I was running, always running. If there was a meeting, I was there. None of this was easy, though. The anxiety of leaving the house and finding people to talk with caused digestive problems throughout the first year. Hearing "our" music on the radio caused belching and churning in my stomach. I solved this by only listening to talk radio.

I tried to combat the restless, sleepless nights with yoga and meditation, in order to rid my body of fatigue and foster the patience that I needed to deal with my new problems. My need for having someone close to me in bed was partially satisfied by hugging my pillow all night.

⊶≪≫⊷

About a month after Joel's death, I began the process of letting go of the physical things we had to live with during the last months of his life.

I put the shower chair away.

I dismantled and stored the raised toilet seat.

I stored the inside walker and the traveling walker.

I called the oxygen people and waited for them to come and take the machine.

I mailed back the scale and special phone apparatus he had been using to contact the center that monitored his diabetes and heart.

I cleaned out his bathroom cabinet and discarded more than thirty bottles of painkillers and medication that nobody else could use.

The effort it took to perform these tasks was, at times, more than I could bear. I smiled when people remarked how well I looked (for a widow). Lifting the walker and wheelchair in and out of the car, caring for Joel's intimate needs, and being constantly on the alert for his comfort had been physically exhausting and certainly hadn't done much for my appearance. I had gone from gaunt to haggard.

At the beginning, what I yearned for most was our daily physical contact, though not in a sexual way. I missed having Joel hold my chair or hold the door open for me, never forgetting his old-fashioned manners. I missed when he stood behind me in line and the body contact that was made, or when he put an arm around my shoulder. Above all, I missed the sweetness of snuggling.

As the months passed, certain positive signs began to appear. I started to visit clothing stores, and some nights I slept until morning. I began to stay home alone in the afternoons. I felt more in tune with my body. Without realizing it, the mourning process was beginning to subside and the healing process was beginning to take effect.

One problem remained, a feeling of anxiety that would rise when I saw something while shopping that brought Joel to mind. Or I would be reminded of something we both loved to do, and my stomach would churn. I realized, however, that the sighing had stopped. The question then became: What was I to do with my life now?

I had never written in a journal or kept a diary, afraid that someone would read my deepest thoughts or desires and know who I really was. Prodded by my daughter and friends, I decided that instead of wallowing in grief at home alone, I would try writing. I joined a writing group, and finding sensitivity, privacy, and a world without criticism, I was able to process a great deal of my grief through the written word.

Week by week, like a tight bud sitting atop the world on a long stem, my words began to open and flower. Feelings, thoughts, and emotions poured out, and believe it or not, I felt better each time I shared the events of life and my feelings of living alone with my small writing group. My writing became a crucial part of my widow's journey.

I was able to ponder such questions as: Did I want to put myself out there (in society) alone? Would I be comfortable with rejection if it occurred? The answers seemed to lie in a re-evaluation of my self-esteem. I decided to give the world a try! Reaching for the outside world helped me feel that my journey was progressing. While I still felt deep grief, it was not as intense or as continuous as in the previous year. I was trying to start a new life—the life I wanted to live.

In order to move ahead, however, I had to realize that self-pity was not the answer. I also had to avoid falling victim to a society that undervalues widows and promotes coupling, whether it be through cruises and vacations designed for lovers, or marketing that forces us buy food packaged for two or more.

I had to reclaim my status as a person who has things to say and who is knowledgeable, articulate, and can stand alone. I had to appreciate the wisdom, experience, and power of widow-hood.

⟨◦⟩

When we moved to California, Joel retired completely. Even after living together for so many years and spending so much time together, that sudden continuous togetherness was not a good plan. As the saying goes, "You cannot have two cooks in one kitchen." We solved this by dividing our responsibilities and time; the mail, the checkbook and finances being relinquished to him.

With Joel gone, my world turned topsy-turvy in a number of ways, not the least of which was dealing with accountants, lawyers, and stockbrokers. Whatever happened to the simplicity of life? I was dominated by the papers I had to review, and compelled to think about the future in a new and foreign way.

At first, everything worked well financially. But then the heavy bills began coming in and cash flow became a problem. I was not a novice at taking care of a checkbook, but after Joel's death I was in for a rude awakening. Suddenly I was drenched in an avalanche of bills. Who *were* these people I had to deal with? I now understand that this is a common occurrence in the first year of widowhood. At the time, however, it caused me much stress.

Gone were the days where Joel would bring home his paycheck and I would divide it up for mortgage, insurance, and food, and then give him his three-dollar allowance for gas, cigarettes, newspapers or anything else he needed. There were weeks when he even brought back change, and this money I squirreled away for gifts and such.

Phone calls had to be made to close accounts that were in Joel's name. Pushing buttons and waiting endless minutes on the phone for the next available person, only to find that I was speaking to the wrong department, or that the office was closed because I forgot the time difference, was frustrating and exhausting for me.

Then there was the paperwork—getting information to the accountant, the lawyer, the stockbroker, looking through an accumulation of records, having the house appraised. All of this financial information had to be amassed to the date of Joel's death in order to satisfy the Internal Revenue Service.

It took a local discount store five months, two lawyers' letters, and a death certificate to eliminate late charges on an account that was closed. It took our auto insurance company three months to close Joel's account and issue one new card to me. It took our credit card company seven months and two death certificates to realize that Joel's account was closed and to stop sending late charges.

During this havoc I realized that the simplicity of life was lost in cubicles. Each person I spoke to was probably encased in his or her own cubicle, furnished with a chair, a phone, and a computer. He or she was unable to think outside their box. No question could be stressed beyond a point, and at that point I was told, "Hold on, I will direct you to another department." And so I went on and on in circles until I finally found the right department, sometimes taking hours and days on the phone.

While the frustrations of daily life preyed upon me, the feelings of vulnerability, weariness, and loneliness were often unbearable. In order to live, life must be shared, and I had lost my beloved.

I went to the accountant and stockbroker, trying very hard to be aware and informed of my financial status. In reality, I needed Joel's wisdom; he would explain our options and a decision would be made. Now I was alone. Luckily for me, our stockbroker and accountant had been in constant touch with Joel, and both assured me that after the first year, money matters would settle down and I would be fairly well off. My accountant even said that if I didn't lose money at the end of the year, it meant that I was not enjoying life as I should. While I appreciated his concern for me, I should not have followed his advice. I was not ready.

I was told that most widows go on a cruise, I forget why. Unable to think for myself, I listened, and in October, two months after Joel's death, I booked a cruise along the Mexican Riviera. After boarding the ship and locating my cabin, I closed the door behind me and broke into incessant sobbing. This occurred every night. I had never been so miserable. There were too many memories of the cruises my darling and I had taken together. I learned that cruises are for couples, not for grieving widows.

When I did the first laundry after Joel's death, I made the decision to discard his underwear and his oversized, over-stretched diabetic socks. I did save some t-shirts, as they make the best rags. To this date, I have not discarded anything else of his. I love to live among his shirts and trousers, his suits and shoes that are gathering dust in our walk-in closet.

It is the World Series. Who do I talk to about the Dodgers and the Giants? With whom do I have great banter as we watch the last of the season games? Joel was a Giants fan, with his Bronx background. I am a Dodgers fan, loyal from the days of the old Brooklyn Dodgers.

I broke my toe getting out of bed in the middle of the night. I was doing a lot of tripping and bumping into things; my feet didn't seem to want to go where my brain sent them. I started to take the portable phone into the bathroom with me when I showered. Fear of falling with nobody around to help, fear of the dark, fear of strange house sounds began to invade my mind. I would check and recheck to make sure all the doors were locked. It took many months for me to calm these anxiety attacks. I still take the phone into the shower with me.

How do you stop the variety of free male catalogues and magazines hawking their wares or glorifying their sales? Don't they know there is no one here to take advantage of their bargains? These constant reminders do nothing but bring anger and resentment to me. With venom, I just heave them into the recycling bin!

In January, I made a New Year's party. I didn't want to drive alone at night, especially that night, so I invited a group of people that Joel and I had known for many years. There were fourteen of us. We had the meal catered. We hired someone to serve and clean up, and with a few glasses of champagne I found myself laughing and even enjoying the evening. But as always, they left and I was alone. Once again, there was no one with whom to exchange the gossip of the evening.

Not until many months after Joel died did I begin to dream about my sweetie. My grief counselor often questioned me about my dreams. I could only answer that I must dream, but had no recollection of the dreams when I awoke. Now I dream about Joel and others who invade our time together, but upon awakening I still cannot remember what the dream was about.

I remember when the three pictures in our living room were taken. They were snapped at three different times in our lives, but are connected by a common thread that runs through them: being on a ship together, on the water. But the missing link is a picture that was never taken, a picture that would connect our lives and make these photos even more meaningful.

How do you take a picture of love? How do you take a picture of peace or contentment? Should we have had a running camera throughout our lives, recording the fun days or the disastrous days? The days we spent on a ship or a boat were among the most gratifying and fruitful of our lives. How do you take a picture of the common bond that connects two people born for each other?

If we were at our happiest floating upon water, is that related to the water in the wombs that nurtured us? Is that how we were destined for each other? How do you take a picture of destiny? I am trying to conceive of a picture that never was, because I don't know how to take a picture that would portray our deep relationship to each other. How do you take a picture of loss, of emptiness?

⟨✦⟩

My emotions were so fragile during the first year that they rode on the tides, going high on the neap tide and slowly out on the ebb. Bills had been settled, there was now no cash flow problem, the mail was not as demanding, and there were no major crises; however, I was—and still am—riding the tide.

Your heart will give you a greater counsel than all the world's scholars.

—Talmud

What keeps me from resting? My mind and body—one seems to work against the other. I have established a weekly routine to take care of the aching pain in my body caused by restlessness and yearning. This pain is not due to any medical problem, but rather to a mindfulness problem. Two days a week I go to a yoga class that helps many of my physical needs and takes away the pain of mind and body, not only by stretching, but by breathing as well. The other days of the week I speed-walk along the ocean and this calms my nerves, thoughts, and body. Resting seems to emerge through physical activity, because it keeps my mind from working, and therefore puts thinking to rest.

At this point in my life, I fear rest and the thoughts that become available to me when I'm not active. I run around all day tiring myself out, so when night comes, I am too tired to think and finally blessed sleep arrives. On the rare occasion that I do sit down to rest, thoughts of my life with Joel crowd into my head, and loneliness and yearning for him bring on the stream of tears. I am not ready to think about the joys we had in life or the finality of death. I have not yet found the middle path where I can find comfort in memories.

Before Joel's death, I could rest. I would just sit in a chair or lie down for half an hour and my mind would be at ease, thinking about the sky or the trees if there was a view, peaceful and comfortable with him at my side. Now in order to rest, I must be active. Through activity I become peaceful.

I light Sabbath candles on Friday nights and try to capture the calmness and the meaning of the Sabbath we had together, but somehow it doesn't work. My mind finds no rest in rest. Rather, restlessness prevails, and I must try to do something else to clear my mind. Activity is the answer, no matter what kind.

I truly yearn for the day when I can find rest for my body and mind, but so far it escapes me. I have tried meditating over and over again, but my mind wanders back to his pain and illness. I understand that time heals all wounds. When will my time come?

∽∾∽

Hello, I'm home! The emptiness of the house echoes back at me. There is no one here to ask me how my day was or to help me carry the bundles of groceries or bargains into the house. I am on my own.

Recently, my daughter Karen and I drove up to Mount Madonna and spent a gloriously peaceful day at this spiritual retreat in the Santa Cruz mountains. Coming home, I needed someone to share this peace with me. A telephone conversation would not do it. *My darling, as always, I needed your presence, your understanding, your arm around my shoulder.*

While I try very hard to make sure that everything is on the table before I sit down for dinner, inevitably I forget something. Some days I am too tired to get up. *This is when I look at your empty chair and ask you for help.* There is no one there and I do without it.

Washing the dishes and cleaning up after a few friends have visited for the evening is the best time for intimate gossip. There is no one there.

A group of us went to see the show "Guys and Dolls" at our local community college. As we walked out singing and laughing, we tried to remember who was in the original cast. *Where were you when I needed you? You would know the answer to this trivia.* There is no one there.

Many times as I sit watching television in the evening I look at the blue chair and ask, "Do you remember that?" or "Do you agree with that?" or "That was really funny, wasn't it?" There is no one there.

So many events occur during a day that would be comforting if you were here to help me with them. Most are just little incidents, sometimes funny, sometimes mind boggling, sometimes thoughtful. But there is no one there.

How many times have I used your strength to open a jar or unscrew a light bulb or move a piece of furniture? Now there is no one there. *I have to be very careful with what I buy. It must be manageable. Your height and strength gave me access to many places that are now unavailable.*

Now, as I open the door to the garage, I call back, *Goodbye, see you later.* Nobody answers, "Be careful." I have lost this dependency and companionship because there is no one there, and that is what it is like to be alone.

Often, as I sit quietly by myself in the late afternoon, I wonder what I should become. What do I hope to become? *How* do I become? These are all questions I need to think about as the aging processes begin to set in. What I am to become is dependent on the possibility of mental health or disability problems.

What do I *hope* to become? I hope to keep my sense of humor and not take myself too seriously, to provide a sense of generation-to-generation for my children and grandchildren, to leave a legacy that I can cope with, even in death, and to support the ability of my children to cope with the death of their parents. This is what I hope to leave behind: a legacy of

hopefulness, of memories sad and happy, for it is within sad-
ness that we learn the true value of happiness.

I have asked my children to name the objects in my house
they feel close to and would like to own. All they do is laugh at
me. They are not ready to name the concrete objects in the
house. I always wonder what gives them the most memories,
and if those memories are pleasurable or stressful. Will these
objects that I leave behind be enough for them?

I hope to leave behind a stable family, one that will continue
generation after generation, with the ability to deal with our
ever-changing world. In these intense times, I wonder.

In my eleventh month of widowhood, it is still not possible
for me to appreciate life. Death of a beloved leaves a void that
cannot be filled. I can fill life with symbols—his bathrobe in the
bathroom, his voice on the answering machine, his favorite shirt
riding beside me in the car—that provide some degree of comfort, but the yearning for a touch, a look, has not subsided.

Life goes on around me. I am surrounded by life. I have a
new great-grandchild on the way. Generations are flowing
through time, but where am I?

While visiting family in Ohio last September, a young
woman came to see me whom I have known for years. She
asked me how I was. Answering in my usual way, I said "Fine,"
knowing that no one really wants to know how you feel; it is
strictly a rhetorical question. She looked me in the eye and said
"How can *you* feel fine when *my* life sucks?" We all burst out
laughing. She and my daughter-in-law dared me to use that line
when next someone asked how I felt.

There were many parties in Ohio and I met many people who inquired how I felt. I couldn't believe that I actually answered two people with "My life sucks." The amazing thing was that it felt good to say that, I got it out, and it was the truth—albeit, I only used the line on people I knew very well. We had a good laugh, it cleared the air, and I felt better for having been honest.

Right now, going through the daily routine of living, I cannot appreciate the life that flows around me, mainly because I have nobody to share the experience with. I am told that the chasm of loneliness will close eventually, but right now the depths of my loneliness have not lessened at all.

Looking back in time, I have gone over our life together again and again. The memories of the good times, the bad times, and then the death, and I am alive and I am blocked. I don't ... I don't ... I don't know what life is all about.

⟡

A dear friend of ours invited me to his eighty-fifth birthday party. The evening before the event, his daughter called. George had had a heart attack and was in the local hospital. Now that he was stabilized, she asked if I would mind coming to his party at the hospital, and I said I would. We had a friendship history. I decided that as a present, I would put together some pictures of the days when his wife and my husband were alive and we socialized as friends. The party would be at 3 p.m. on Wednesday, and his daughter would bring a birthday cake.

When I entered the hospital room, I broke out in a sweat, my mouth went dry and I felt dizzy. There was Joel, not George, in that hospital gown that didn't fit, with one shoulder exposed and hair disheveled. A long-drawn face tried to smile. Tubes were plugged into his arm and the monitor burped behind him. I walked over to the bed, said I had another place to be, excused myself and fled. I could not visit my friend again. I went down to the ocean and grieved for the death of my beloved.

Even in laughter the heart can still ache.

—Proverbs 14:13

While taking a shower one rainy morning, I realized that bit by bit the essence of my beloved was dissolving into air, with the use and disuse of the things we shared. He could not use his shower because the tub was too narrow for the shower chair. We shared my stall shower, but now the chair had been put away. The soap we shared had recently melted; the shampoo we shared had been gone for two months. The powder and the common bathroom his-and-her cosmetics had all been replaced. *Your touch was no longer on them.* Joel has left my bathroom.

When living together, sharing is one of the joys of life. It is the bonding of faith and gratitude for each other. *The cereal, the tea, all the staples we shared have been used up, and those we didn't are now in disuse.*

Now, at this time in my widowhood, the use and disuse in our lives sometimes seems to fade. Other times, the yearning for Joel causes an awful jolt in the stomach and churning in the whole digestive system. When I use his desk, memories come flooding back, a dam broken upstream that cannot be contained. His robe is in the bathroom and his chair is in the family room (a little tattered, he used it well); these two objects, the bathrobe I embrace in the morning and evening and the chair I sit in to open the mail (his fingers were not nimble enough and there was pain), still provide a sanctuary for me.

My sweetie, you never sat in our new car. I sold the Matrix and the Mercedes and had the notorious police drama in our new car. There is no sense of you in the Camry. Where have you gone? I miss you so. Do you know that I now sit in the computer chair and use e-mail and Google? Your password is gone and there is a new address, but only a catastrophe will eliminate your voice from the answering machine, or your blue bathrobe from the bathroom where you died in my arms.

Joel, your airline miles have been transferred to my account. I had to send a death certificate to verify that you were no longer a part of my life. I canceled your credit card when I had to pay a fee to renew it. You are disappearing physically from my life.

So please, nobody judge me when I leave his voice on the answering machine, or wonder why his bathrobe is still in the bathroom. Don't judge me, the one left behind—understand and support me.

⚬⚬⚬

I have to learn to live with loneliness and emptiness, and go on from there to make a life. How do I make a life for myself from this point? *I have to learn to live with friends and yet, have no one true friend such as you, dearie.* I have to learn to go out alone, aware that no one knows where I am or what I am doing.

The loneliness of not being able to relate to a special person, telling tales of where you have been or what you have done—this is what I must learn to live with. On the outside my life seems full, surrounded by family, friends, and projects. But on the inside, the emptiness cannot be filled. After all this time, the loneliness and emptiness still persist.

⚬⚬⚬

When you were with me, my darling, I could do anything. No task was too great. "Me woman," I would joke, as I would flex my flaccid muscles. Now I have time, and no great medical issues to deal with, but, as the song says, "Is this all there is to life?"

What happens in between the activities, what fills the silences of the days and nights that I am experiencing? I don't want to think too deeply, that frightens me. How far into eternity do I dare explore? *Are you there, my darling?*

All of these thoughts ran rampant through my mind as I sat on the bus, on the way to the Legion of Honor Museum in San Francisco to see the Monet exhibit. The bus shuddered along the uneven road, filled with the incessant chattering of the women, one speaking louder than the other in order to be heard above the noise. Words came at me, dangling in the cacophony of sounds. My seatmate and I were silent.

Would you have taken this trip with me? There were a few reluctant men accompanying their wives, silently reading their papers, unwilling to get into the fray. Perhaps in earlier years we would have sat together, thighs touching, silent in our own thoughts, no need to speak, but together.

At the museum there were pictures of the water lilies at Giverny. I tried to put myself into the moment when we strolled through those gardens and were thoroughly awed by the quiet and beauty of the scene, inhaling the air, trying to see what Monet saw.

When I came home from the museum I delved into our picture albums and sure enough, there we were in Monet's garden. What joy, what memories I was filled with! Then, sitting in your blue chair, I opened the mail and read, "The Yahrzeit (anniversary of the death according to the Jewish calendar) of your beloved, Joel Zelin, will fall on August 4, 2006. In observance of the Yahrzeit, his name will be read and Kaddish (prayer for the dead) recited at services August 11, 2006."

I could not eat dinner this night. The knotted rope returned.

Then there was some light ...

While browsing through greeting cards, I came across one that pictured a half-full glass, a half-empty glass, and a glass filled with a denture. *Oh sweetie, what fun we would have had with this card, and especially the denture glass! How your sons and grandchildren would have enjoyed pictures of our dentures in a glass.* The denture glass had become an inside family joke. Every time we visited we needed two glasses in the bathroom, a circumstance to be taken with humor and sensitivity.

But what about the other glasses? In the last two years of your life, how did your glass look? I don't know how you endured the endless pain you were always encumbered with, as each portion of your body erupted at different times. There was never a truce between pain and your body. My darling, when I cleaned out your medicine chest there were so many plastic bottles of various painkillers. How did you endure it? Throughout all of this, with constant reminders on my part that your glass was half full, your spirit survived and we progressed day by day.

Our glass was never half empty. Our daughter and her family gave us laughter and a feeling that each day brought a new adventure. Miles of country kept our sons apart but the visits were frequent and the phone calls regular. Yes darling, our family kept our glass half full.

Our life together was an adventure even as your body deteriorated. We had each other. We made plans to travel on a cruise ship that would provide you with your regular routine of dialysis. We went out to dinner, we saw friends. Yes, our glass was half full.

Both physically and socially we took care of each other. We shared intimacies the best we could until the very end. We enjoyed each other's company at all times. My strength would never allow bitterness to enter our home. Even as we ran to the E.R. almost daily, I continued to assure you that even with all these glitches, we

*still came home to a half-full glass. I kept showing you that
my strength and your endurance would keep us together.*

*Even in death your glass was half full. Death came suddenly; I
felt your body relax in my arms and I believe you smiled as the pain
finally left.*

*Your funeral was a tribute to you and your life, evidenced by the
number of people who attended. Even in death your glass was half
full. As the months passed, people did not forget, and the same tribute was awarded you at your unveiling ceremony.*

Yes, my beloved, we have always had a half-full glass to share.

Who is the blessing in my life? In this period of time, I would
not have been able to survive without my daughter. In these
past few months, we have cried together, reminisced together,
sat quietly together, and just been there for one another,
together.

Every morning the phone call breaks through the silence of
the house and instinctively I know who is at the other end. I am
blessed to have someone to discuss the day with me, someone
who cares where I am going, someone who cares what I have
seen, what made me sad, what made me happy.

I didn't want to make my daughter my sounding board
because she has so many things in her life. I didn't want to burden her with my problems. I am blessed because she ignored my
continued protests and insisted on becoming a daily part of my
life.

I am blessed with her goodness and her intuitiveness. She
steered me to a writing class and insisted on my visiting a grief
counselor in a one-on-one encounter. I am blessed because we

have overcome our past mother-daughter problems and con-
frontations. We have developed a mutual friend/counselor/wis-
dom of the young/wisdom of the old relationship that is truly
comfortable for both of us.

My daughter made an interesting comment today, while we
were waiting for the Fourth of July parade to begin. She said I
was a "free agent," meaning that I could come and go whenever
I wanted to. That evening, I started to think about being a free
agent, and how it really concerned me. I couldn't get the idea
out of my head. Am I free—free from what?

Am I free to stay cozy in bed every morning and arise to start
the day whenever I am ready? Then why do I have such restless
nights, and wake at the crack of dawn looking to snuggle, finding no one there, and rolling out of bed to start another long
day?

Am I free from the responsibility of washing, cooking, shopping, and taking care of another person—in exchange for sitting
around a lonely house, making plans a week in advance so that
every day is occupied?

Am I free because I can do anything on a whim, anything I
care to, without consulting the opinion of another person?

Am I free to hold the television clicker and change the station
whenever I want? Then why, when it's not in use, do I hand it
back to the blue chair?

*Am I free to dress the way I want because you are not there to
say, "How beautiful you are in my eyes"?*

Am I free to put the heat up whenever I want and not worry that someone will turn it down? Then why have I suddenly become so conscious of conservation?

Are my clothes free as they cycle their way through the washer and dryer, no longer bothered by the extra-tall large size clothing they had to tumble with? Do they feel free in a unisex environment?

Am I free, or has the rhythm of my life changed? My hours have changed in order to accommodate my friends, the single women and married women who have other responsibilities. In order to meet with anyone, I am using hours I never scheduled when my sweetie was alive. Does this make me freer, or am I just entering another life rhythm, and only *appear* to be a free agent?

Since your death, I have had to make many choices, cope with many problems. Notwithstanding all of this, my biggest effort will be to encompass the problem of how to change the rhythm of my life while still holding on to you, sweetie.

Am I free? *The only thing I am free from is you, my darling, and as a free agent I must learn to live with what it really means to be free ... and alone.*

Joel, sweetie, I don't know what is happening to me. Your Unveiling is in one week and the nearer we get to Sunday, the more depressed I become. Today, while taking my walk along the beach, the dry sobbing suddenly started again. I don't know where it came from. As that friend said, "I feel fine, but my life sucks." The abysmal loneliness is still with me.

I went to Rachel's graduation and had to change planes in Chicago. I stopped for a moment at the place you first rested when you had your heart attack. My mind became a turmoil of memories. I was completely absorbed in thoughts of you.

My stay in Akron was warm and friendly. Your great-grandchild Noah would have given you many pleasurable moments. I came home through Dallas, again assailed by memories of how difficult it was for you to get from terminal to terminal using that driverless train. It is so difficult to explain the depth of my feeling upon returning home to an empty house.

Today I planted the annuals to give color to the backyard. We always had such pleasure sitting in the family room looking out at the summer blooms. You would laugh so when all of a sudden I would race out the door, trying to frighten away the squirrels that dug up my plants. We would share our orange and at times you would join me in a Lillet before dinner.

These were the times when I would sit on your lap to cut your nails and you would grimace and moan, afraid I would cut your finger and the bleeding would start. I never did cut your fingers. In times like this your rash would be sharp with pain and I would apply salve to your body. Along with the relief, you would melt with joy as I rubbed your back. We were so intimate in these treasured moments.

In these past months I have tried to block out those daily routines that kept us absorbed in each other. But lately the wall I have built around me seems to be crumbling as I sit here writing, looking for you in your blue chair. I cannot alleviate the pain and grief resulting from your death, and the tears flow again.

What I am trying to tell you, my beloved, my deeply beloved, is that the defensive wall built by inuring my deepest thoughts and feelings is beginning to crumble. As your stone is about to be unveiled, so are my defenses, and coming slowly to the surface is the realization of the never-ness *of death: never to feel, never to touch, never to smell, never to hear, never to see you again.*

⸻

Sweetie, it is time for the Unveiling of your gravestone. I chose this date and your children agreed, because it is your birthday and it is Father's Day. Once more, in keeping with the Jewish tradition, I am sitting at your graveside. The official mourning period is over. The wail of the clarinet wafts gently through the air; your friends and family surround you. The Rabbi's intonation of the prayers is lyrical and sweet. Finally, the unveiling of the gravestone, then the placing of small stones so that your spirit will know we were there. All of these ceremonies handed down through the centuries.

If this is the end of the mourning period, is there closure? Your sons are relieved of the duty to recite the Kaddish prayer every day—is it closure for them? Your daughter has mourned in her own way, is there closure for her?

As I sit here writing, my body feels weary. The depths of my emotions and the agony of the effort to keep them under control are, I feel at times, wearing me out. And yet each time something occurs and stirs a memory of our life together, it hits a chord deep within me and another layer of my sorrow is unveiled.

Closure? Not yet. But I do feel I can walk out of the caverns of pity, solitude and darkness that I have endured these last ten months and emerge into a maze of color: high hedges, blue sky, and various paths to take as I try to find my way through memories. Sweetie, do you remember the many years we traveled and visited chateaus, castles and palaces, and admired the mazes from the second-floor windows? How we joked when we tried to distinguish a castle from a palace from a chateau? We finally put them all together and called them passales.

That is where I am now, reflecting and talking to myself, at the second-floor window gazing down at my spiritual body as it floats through the daze, haze, maze, turning corners, looking for what? I don't know—surrender to my new life, a release of weariness, to stop smiling as if everything was all right, perhaps to discover if closure is what I really want.

The Unveiling has caused me to question if I really want closure. Could it be that my problem stems from this questioning? Coming out of the caves of darkness, I realize that closure could cancel all memories; closure could eliminate our past life by encircling it out of the present. Closure could seal you away.

No, closure is not what I desire. I want a way out of the caverns of solitude and darkness, a way out of the maze with the glorious memories of the past. As these memories soften and ease, I believe I will mellow and will find comfort in this mellowness.

Thus, emerging from the cavern, blinking into the light of the maze, discovering the path out of the maze, and surrounding myself with the physical objects you have left behind (your voice on the answering machine, your blue chair, your blue bathrobe, your shirt riding beside me in the car), all of these will endear and unveil the memory of our relationship, and with time unveil another plateau I have surmounted.

Our love is eternal.

In the rising sun and in its going down,
we remember them.
In the blowing of the wind and in the chill of winter,
we remember them.
In the opening of buds and in the rebirth of spring,
we remember them.
In the blueness of the sky and in the warmth of summer,
we remember them.
In the rustling of the leaves and in the beauty of autumn,
we remember them.
In the beginning of the year and when it ends,
we remember them.
When we are weary and in need of strength,
we remember them.
When we are lost and sick at heart,
we remember them.
When we have joys we yearn to share,
we remember them.
So long as we live, they too shall live, for they are now a part of
us as we remember them.

—the Mourners' Kaddish

The origins of the Mourners' Kaddish are lost in time. Many
variations of the Kaddish exist today. This version is used for
memorial services.

It is July 2006, and a year of our past lives together has slipped by. No more can I reminisce about this time last year. The end of summer became fall and fall became winter, then spring and now summer. No more can I compare this year with the events of last year that we shared together. A new year has started.

This time last year we cruised to Alaska. You needed a walker and a wheelchair to maneuver more easily around the ship. This time last fall, we went to our first great-grandchild's circumcision. You stayed in bed the entire weekend. Fall became winter and the visits to doctors became more frequent. We went to a lodge located on the Monterey Bay for a weekend with our daughter and her family. You began to use a wheelchair more often. Your knees were giving way. We avoided many places that had steps. Last year we celebrated New Year's Eve with our Chavurah in our home, because you were more comfortable there than away.

In the spring we went to an Elderhostel. We started to entertain at home, it was easier for you. In the late spring you had the catheter inserted near your right shoulder so that the two leads for dialysis would be external permanently, to prevent hemorrhaging. If they put a shunt into your arm, the two leads had to be inserted each time, and with your blood problem this was a risk. You started dialysis a week later. During the early summer we planned a cruise on a ship that would accommodate your dialysis routine.

In August last year, every Thursday we savored our lunch at a diner after your dialysis, even though you were very tired. I know you did this for me, to spare me working in the kitchen for at least that meal.

This time last year your body was wearing down too rapidly. You found it difficult to get out of bed. You sat at the sink to towel-wash your body from shoulder to waist. You could not wet the exposed leads for fear of infection. I washed your back and your hair *in the sink. This time last year you sat in a chair in the shower to wash the lower part of your body. I helped. This time last year, the pain you always endured was becoming incredibly intense.*

In the early summer of last year we found a buttonhook for you to use. Your fingers could not close the buttons on your shirt and you wanted to be a little more independent. You looked so sweet as you worked the button into the hole, concentrating so hard, accomplishing a task. Thank goodness you were able to zip a zipper. We laughed at that.

This time last year, until August 25th, it was always we, we, we. Now my journey continues and it is I, I, I.

According to the Jewish calendar it is one year since your death, but in reality the days have been one long endless procession—time had no meaning, days had no meaning. Tonight the Rabbi read your name aloud in the Temple, and when it came time to recite the prayer for the departed I stood up. Remember how we used to count tissues? Tonight was an eight-tissue night. As each of the major prayers were said throughout the service, the tears started to flow. I remembered how we stood together and recited them, your strong voice loud and clear, reciting each prayer in Hebrew. You really enjoyed the Jewish tradition and the feeling of peace and family closeness you found, both with your family and with the Temple family in these services.

Now, being part of this Temple family, a friend sitting next to me put her arm around my shoulder during the service and this gave me great comfort. Going to this service was one of the hardest things I have had to do since your death. I thought that I had my emotions under control, but for the last few days I have felt jittery, distressed, and sometimes even abandoned. *How will I feel in two days, when I have to light your memorial candle? Will this tradition have a meaning?*

We were so strong together; we were one. I want that again, but know that it can never be. Learning to live with memories has been most difficult. I don't want memories, I want you! I want the fun we had together; I want the enjoyment of life back again. I have tried so hard to sublimate these feelings but tonight they came out in full force. Maybe this night was good for me. I let all of my emotions hang out again and maybe tomorrow I will feel better. The head-ache will go away, and there will be meaning.

Today is Sunday, the night I light your memorial candle. There is heaviness on my chest and my voice has lost its "up tone." Outside the fog is heavy, the morning gray, and recollections of last year at this time invade, a relentless army of ants digging deeper and deeper into my heart. As I pass the mirror I realize I am dressed in black. A friend called and asked if I wanted company when I lit the candle. Thanking her, I declined. It was a time for privacy.

When I think about this year, I think that the term "merry widow" is a myth. Sometime during the past year there may have been a small cranny that at times widened a drop to allow a little bit of subdued enjoyment to enter, but "merry" was never felt.

The memorial candle is on the counter, and as I walk by it all afternoon my emotions are in a rampage. I don't want to light it—I have to light it—is it the end or the beginning of a new stage for me? Will I be able to find some meaning in my life now? We needed more time together, healthy or sick doesn't matter, we would be together. *Am I lighting this for you, my sweetie, or for me?*

It is evening and the candle is lit. How do I feel? Numb, without feeling, sober, quiet. What is there to feel? Everything is final and I must learn to live with the finality of the truth as I sit down to endless days of lonely dinners and lonely nights.

Oh my darling, what great joy in our family today! We have become great-grandparents again. I can just feel the great pride you would have felt if you were here, and I can hear all the phone calls you would have made. You would have informed everyone you saw all about your new family member and your love of family.

In all the excitement, I nearly forgot to tell you that the baby is a girl, weighing in at seven pounds, ten ounces. We have so much for which to be grateful. One of the many things is the thoughtfulness of all our grandchildren; in addition to regular phone calls, our granddaughter Erin sends regular updated pictures of Noah, our first great-grandchild, on the computer. Two weeks ago she sent pictures of Noah's first haircut. He was just two years old and now he looks like such a big boy.

Sweetie, why did you leave us so soon? Your pride in our growing family would have caused your happiness to expand to the extent that it may have eased the daily pain you lived with.

The best news is that they named the baby Sadie Joelle—so there you are, my beloved, you and your name exist in the next generation.

P.S. And yes, my darling, I did send a notice to the Temple newsletter informing everyone of the birth, and yes, I called your sister in Florida.

⟨∞⟩

The distance between us shifts from day to day. There are days when you are close to me in my actions and thoughts, especially when I awaken. Memories engulf my mind as I wander through the daily routine of greeting your pillow in the morning, of wrapping my face in your bathrobe that hangs in the bathroom and retains your odor. I wonder, after all these months, how much longer until your scent, too, becomes a memory.

As I go through the routine of the day, memories return with a jolt back to you, my darling: how we enjoyed going to the Mended Hearts meetings on Wednesdays, talking to friends and savoring lunch together before the speaker started. How we took pleasure in our daily trip to the coffee shop at 3 p.m., meeting the same acquaintances and arguing or discussing stories of musicians during the 40s or 50s, sports figures current and past, or war stories that became more glorious as time went on. The distance between us was short on the days we came home around 4 p.m., read the mail together, and shared our orange. We had to share because you were not supposed to eat citrus fruit, but we rationalized that it whet the appetite and that a few pieces couldn't really hurt. These times were so precious to us, as we discussed the day's mail and gossiped about the people we saw that day.

Then there are days when memory fails me, and I don't know where you are in my life now. I have tried to make a life for myself by joining a yoga class, art and writing classes, any opportunity to leave the house daily and interact with people. I just keep going at every opportunity that arises. Am I trying to distance myself from you? Many times during these days I feel lost, no matter how busy I am. I feel as if I am floundering around, looking for a base of some

*kind. Not until I return to the confines of my home do I feel
grounded and secure.*

*What is the distance between us? Am I better off shortening or
lengthening the distance? I have no answer.*

⚬

Maybe I will find inside happiness by reinventing myself.
Now that life is only about me, without someone to love inti-
mately (only memories), the question I ask myself is "*What is
my potential?*" If I were an organization or a group, I would
probably publish a mission statement. I am seventy-nine years
old and have been forced to start a new life. Since my mourning
and grieving are becoming less frequent, shouldn't my spirit be
freer? What happens now? How do I go about starting a new
life? So many questions without answers.

I have tried to step back and look at myself and my place in
the circle of friends and family that surround me; still I feel
lonely. When will the day come that I can be a person with a
purpose in life other than myself?

I do not want to become so self-centered that I don't recog-
nize the world around me. I must stop running, looking for
things to do, looking for any kind of companionship. I look for
the day when I can settle down and find peace and comfort
within myself. *This will be my inside happiness, and my beloved, I
will take you with me.*

⚬

*Well, dearie, I am fifteen months into widowhood. The depth
of the loneliness remains constant, but I do see certain changes in*

attitude. *This week I started to listen to the "Golden Oldies" radio station. Until now I could not bear to hear the songs we grew up on together and loved so much. I must admit I had to change the station after a few songs, as the feelings were too intense. But I guess it is the start of something in my mind, body, and soul—is it the beginning of letting go?*

Another interesting thing happened to me this Thanksgiving weekend. I met someone who asked if I had a picture of my husband in my wallet. I shook my head no. When I got home, I took out the photo albums. It was time to put a picture of us in my wallet. I chose one from 1983, before the onset of your illnesses. We were young, had money in our pockets, and our children were making their way through the world. They were good children and I guess we had it all, and the picture showed it. Until now I have not been able to look at pictures of you, of us. The hurt of your death, and before that, your illness, was still unbearable.

Am I starting to let go? Am I learning to live without you? When will the loneliness disappear? It seems I feel the need to immerse myself in you, now more than ever. Is that the reason for the songs, the pictures? I need more evidence of you around me. Fifteen months!—what a hellish ride it has been.

Then there was life ...

Entering my second year of widowhood, I started to feel restless and felt the need to try something different, to get away from the routine of my daily life. When a brochure arrived in the mail describing a trip to China that included Shanghai, cruising on the Yangtze River, exploring the villages and towns along the way, and ending in Beijing, I decided to risk it. Perhaps it would not be as disastrous as the trip to Mexico the previous year.

As the date of departure drew near, I knew that I needed to be well-rested. Without sleep I was completely useless and thoughtless. The trip would entail an eleven-hour flight from San Francisco Airport to Narita Airport in Tokyo, with a four-hour layover before I boarded a plane for the three-hour trip to Shanghai, my final destination. It would be a day without sleep, a day or night of walking around strange airports, unable to read the language—a day of utter confusion and disorientation.

Knowing from many years of travel how unsteady I am on my feet after any length of time on a plane, the decision was made—I would call for wheelchair assistance! I put aside my dignity and pride and succumbed to the decision, which turned out to be one of the wisest I have ever made.

All of the people who pushed the different wheelchairs were very solicitous, from holding my arm while I got into the seat, to lifting each leg very gently before putting them on the foot-rests—the same legs that only yesterday were speed walking along the ocean. Little did they know that at any other time, I was capable of running alongside that wheelchair. But that was not the time for pride.

I knew how to enter an elevator backwards, so that it was easier to push the chair out at the necessary floor. About five years ago I became the official pusher when Joel had his first heart attack and his knees began to deteriorate. I became part of the brigade of caretakers who pushed their spouses through the endless marble corridors of airports, looking for the restroom and the designated gate. Not until you become one of these women do you see them—or if you do see them, you avert your gaze. Once I joined this group, we looked into each others' eyes as we passed, never saying a word but the camaraderie was there, knowing that this phase of becoming old and the hardship that both parties endure were part of the process.

How did I feel the first time I was helped into that wheelchair? The one who practices yoga two or three times a week and speed walks for two miles at least five times a week, the one who is trying to delay the aging process as best I can, how did I feel? *Old.* As soon as I sank into that chair, my shoulders scrunched up to my ears and I felt as if I had lost my dignity and my ability to perform in a vital situation. I succumbed to old age.

As I was pushed from gate to gate, people either averted their eyes or smiled at me with a sympathetic look. All of a sudden I was too tired to fight back. As I sat in that wheelchair in different airports, I thought about the elderly people in rest homes and hospitals who sit waiting listlessly, day after day, for someone to come and push them somewhere else. What is it that we who can move around feel when we look at elderly people? Is it fear that one day our turn will come?

The upside of being pushed through an airport is that everyone makes way for you, and you are always first in line. I guess that was some compensation for the loss of dignity and pride that I felt.

Yes, it was a wise decision I made. When I finally reached Singapore I was very unsteady on my feet from the lack of sleep.

When traveling alone, any new situation takes on an enormous proportion of difficulty—I think because as I get older, the fear of falling takes precedence over everything else.

⸲⸙⸰

And Adonai told Noah to gather all creatures, great and small, and two by two they entered the Ark. This is the beginning of couples or coupling. When you travel alone you are an extra wheel at a table set for ten or twelve. You have an extra empty seat beside you on the bus trips. Whether heterosexual, gay, or lesbian, a couple is always more readily accepted than a single person.

The air in Shanghai, and all along the Yangtze River, must be heavily polluted. Our driver and guide repeatedly reminded us of what beautiful sunny days we were having. I knew the sun was up there, but the haze obliterated it. All I could see was a dim, faraway yellow circle. My eyes burned constantly, my nose ran, and I sneezed repeatedly. It must have been the pollution in the air. What puzzled me, however, was that I was having that allergic reaction whether we were traveling through dense urban areas or green countryside.

In the next reincarnation, I must have my plumbing changed. I realized this for the first time when I was young and traveling through Europe. On the road in China, while the bathrooms were not slits in the ground and were fairly clean, they were still what we call "eastern style," and squatting was the only way to eliminate. Even with years of yoga, that still presented a problem.

Sweetheart, today we were taken to a factory that manufactures fine china and porcelain. They still use the hundreds-of-years-old process of turning the wheel by foot and hand to shape the pieces. Then we were led to the kiln, and finally to the room where everything is packaged. You would have had a grand time talking with the management, because the final packaging was a red cardboard valise box with a handle and sides, just like the ones you used to manufacture in New York. They also packaged the pieces in boxes in which the top was held on by ribbons attached to the side. You would have had so much to talk about, and would have reminisced about the old days in the box business. Oh, how I wish you were here. My eyes welled up with tears as I opened the boxes that I recognized from my past life with you.

As the days passed we went from bazaar to bazaar, and I had no desire to buy anything! I felt as if I had been there, done that, and we didn't need anything else in the house. While all the couples around me were buying and accumulating as we once did, I just thought of us and our good times, and smiled with tears in my eyes.

What is it that I needed as I sailed aboard a ship on the Yangtze River? The food was decent and I had the most unbelievable back massage—but what is it that I needed?

I needed that feeling of loneliness deep down in my heart, if not to go away, maybe just to mellow out and not be as intense. I needed someone to care when I left the cabin, to ask when I would return and to greet me when I did. I needed someone at my side as I watched the most beautiful sunrise one morning. I needed someone to hum along with me as they played the old Frank Sinatra records.

I need you, my darling, just to sit by my side or to nudge me so that I can feel your closeness, and when you died, sweetheart, my need became overwhelming.

⟨✑⟩

Sweetie, now when I travel I must always remember to bring some part of you with me. This time, on my Yangtze River trip, I took the belt from your blue terrycloth bathrobe and put it on the pillow next to me when I went to sleep. In this way we have pillow talk.

Now when I travel I have to figure out how to use all of the appliances: how to turn on the water in the modern shower, how to turn the lights on and off in the cabin, and more essentially, how to open child-proof supplies I brought for the trip. You would never believe Chinese sink stoppers! In order to raise and lower the stopper in the bathroom, you use your thumb to press it up or down in the center. This stumped many people.

Now when I travel I must enjoy the sights alone. Although everyone is very nice about including me in their conversations, I do not have the intimacy of your presence.

Now when I travel I am responsible for figuring out the money exchange. One of the kind young gentlemen explained that if I divide by eight, I'll be able to estimate the amount in dollars.

Now when I travel I have to deal with the safe in the clothes closet. You would be so proud of me! I figured out how to put in my number code to open the safe, and how to close it. You know that following these directions is not my forté.

Five days into the trip, my usual sore throat and cold developed, likely caused by the air conditioning on the plane. Some things never change, though many others do.

Now I have no one to share the experience of buying souvenirs, or the adventure of searching and finding the perfect gift.

Now I never lock the strange bathroom doors. There is always the fear that I will not be able to unlock them and nobody will come looking for me or wonder what is taking me such a long time.

While I am traveling, people call out, "Gilda, come join us." (When you are in a group, you wear name tags.) After a while there is always the question, "Where is your partner?" The answer, "I am traveling alone." The comment, "Oh!" The emptiness of the chair next to me is so evident around the coupled table that all conversation across the table stops and only the murmuring between couples is heard.

I have tried to avoid the couples who are not really partners. These are the women who, for financial reasons mainly, decide to travel with either a friend or with someone the tour provided for them. These are the women who sit back with blank faces, trying to look around but who, in reality, are probably thinking of their past lives. These are the women who are on the tour because their family insisted they get away. These women are unhappy with themselves and with life, and cannot find a way out of their unhappiness.

These are the widows who have no place in our society. They float on the outside of every social event. I will not be part of this group. I will be accepted as I am, alone, or I will function in my own world, involved with the world—as Frank Sinatra sang, I'll do it my way.

While I am traveling, I have to be my own partner. As every cook needs a *sous chef*, every traveler needs someone to be counted upon to help carry the daily needs, including camera, binoculars, water, and information for daily excursions. I must be responsible for remembering all of the essentials that will make my day more pleasant. There is no one to share the checklist—no one to blame for forgetting something—no one to discuss the upcoming event with, or to recount it at day's end.

While I am traveling, I am the world. There is no one to depend upon. I am a free spirit, for better or for worse. I am determined to enjoy what I have as long as I have it, as long as the memory of my love comes with me.

Will I continue to travel? Only time will tell. *But wherever I go, in some way, you will be with me always.*

In retrospect

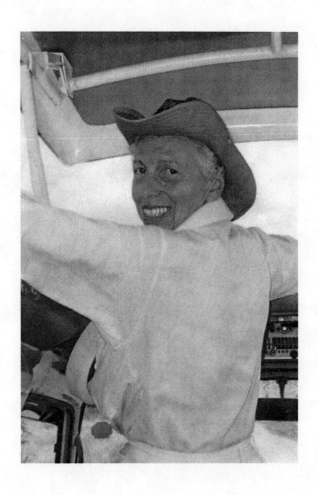

Four or five mornings during the week I visit my psychiatrist. I hop into my car, drive down to the beach, and enter my psychiatrist's office: the ocean. It is on these walks, as the sun is rising over the mountains and the ocean is sparkling, that I can truthfully confide. I talk and cry about events, problems, issues, family and friends, knowing that all of this is confidential, for I have found my ocean to be noncommittal and forgiving.

The beauty of the sea as it crashes to the beach allows me the peace of mind I need to go on. There are no issues here. Here there is truth and beauty to fill all senses of my body. I keep the conversation going and the water washes over my mind. It bathes and clears my thoughts and the mornings of my life become more bearable. As I walk back to my car cleansed and refreshed, a new day dawns full of hope, and by the evening, maybe the emptiness will be soothed for that day.

The afternoons of my life rush by as I try to deal with life commitments. What can I accomplish during the day that will make me content by the evening? The visits to the grocery and drug store satisfy my physical survival needs, but the most fulfilling times are the coffee shop talks with friends. They know and understand me. I am imbued with a feeling of deep relaxation when I leave them.

There are the days I give service to the community by working for organizations like Senior Connections, Hospice, or the gift shop in the Temple, but sometimes I wonder: Do they work for me or do I work for them? These activities and appointments are a destination, an excuse to leave the house, knowing that I will find companionship. I have found that the rewards of putting yourself out there far outweigh sitting at home in a well of loneliness.

As the days go by, I feel that I have now entered the evening of my life, and as the sky becomes a fiery red and the ocean dark and foreboding, I look back to how I have related to family, friends, and acquaintances. Would I have done anything differently? One of my dearest friends is in the last stages of lung cancer and another has just lost her husband. A man I know has been diagnosed with colon cancer. Is this what the evening of my life will be?

Then I turn to my children and grandchildren. I look forward to the good news of their accomplishments. The news runs from winning a soccer game to acing college finals to summer travel plans to boyfriends. Their lives are filled with expectations and hope. The expanse of their dreams keeps my spirit alive and fills the evenings of my life.

Not taking myself too seriously when I talk to my family eases tensions and guilt feelings they may have due to the physical distance between us. My grandchildren love to talk about their grandmother who does headstands in yoga, goes salmon fishing, and travels all over the world when she can. These memories preserve my sense of aliveness as I travel through the morning, to the afternoon, and into the evening of my life.

My darling, this is the second Thanksgiving without you. We all miss you so. While I was cooking Thanksgiving dishes to bring to our daughter's house, how I missed your sniffing around the kitchen, taking in all the assorted odors, trying to taste everything, offering advice—oh, how annoyed I used to be! I would give a great deal to have you accompany me to Karen and Bill's house, where you and Karen would fight over the tuchus of the turkey, and you and Bill would sit and discuss wine and food. We lifted a glass of champagne in your honor, but we needed your huge presence.

Every day during this long four-day weekend I walk along the beach reminiscing about our life together: how we gathered the family together when we were young, the times we celebrated Chanukkah during Thanksgiving because everyone lived so far apart. The gossiping, the talking quietly, and the togetherness did our hearts good as we watched our family grow, year by year.

Now I am alone. There is no one to talk to, no sounding board for my ideas or impressions, so I talk aloud to you, sweetie. I am very lucky that I can call our daughter. She has a willing ear for me; she lets me talk on and on, only giving an opinion when I ask for it and never criticizing. That ready ear is there for me every day. I am truly blessed that we have a daughter who listens so patiently, and who understands my loneliness.

_∞

Sweetie, I visited your grave today. The weeds were overtaking the site, and since there is no perpetual care in this cemetery I hired a gardener to do some landscaping. I was very pleased with the way he placed the slate, interspersed with low thyme and California drought-resistant plants. Alongside the headstone, he planted a rhododendron tree. We also put in "naked lady" bulbs for you to enjoy as they blossom in August.

Instead of a visit full of tears or sobbing, I found that I was more reflective. Calmly, my mind dwelled on past memories of our life together, and how death is also a part of living.

Joel, you are still with me when I speak your name, even in my despair. How can I grieve when I know the pain you were in? Your death has diminished me so because you were part of my life, but you are *still a part of me as long as I can write and tell tales of our life as it was.*

And then, I can even go on, someday, on my own, for I have grieved, I have mourned. I will always remember and be glad for what we had. Your death did not destroy the years we had together, but rather has caused me to celebrate them in writing. This is our gift for our children.

When I came home, I realized I had reached a new plateau in my life as it is now. While there is no true feeling of contentment, I do not harbor as deep a feeling of abandonment as I had earlier. I am getting used to coming home to an empty house. Rather than raging about my loneliness, I have become more accepting. I am learning to deal with each situation that confronts me without falling apart, whether they test my ineptitude at fixing basic things around the house, my feelings of impatience, or just dealing with events in my daily routine.

Now I have to think about what I want, not what I think other people want of me. I feel that I have about ten more years of good living. What do I *want to do with those years?*

Sweetie, I went out early this morning for my walk along the beach. It is so much more beautiful to walk in the fog with the mist dropping on my face and the denseness wrapping around me, sometimes heavily, sometimes lightly, depending on how the wind is blowing.

While walking, I realized that this was another "this time last year" day. Today is June 17, 2007 and this is the day last year that we unveiled your gravestone. Another year has passed and my life goes on. You are very present in my thoughts during my walks along the beach. This is when we do our best reminiscing together and try to solve any problems that exist in my life.

One thing that is really bothering me, dearie, is that nobody wants to talk about you. Don't they realize how I would love to hear any stories that relate to you? How comforting it would be for me to hear these stories, maybe get a good laugh or learn something about you from the past, or just engage in good conversation, remembering when this or that happened. Why can't your family or your friends talk about you? Is your death still so hurtful, or are they shy, not knowing how I will react?

Maybe in the future I will take the initiative and see where that leads. I still have to learn to cope with the world around me, and all the unanswered questions that confront me.

⚘

My nights have been very restless lately. I am waking up every two hours or so, twisting and turning continually. Through my early morning lethargy, I realized that tomorrow will be two years since my beloved's death. I cannot refer to the date as an anniversary. Anniversaries are for parties, family get-togethers, and special dinners. How did my subconscious mind and body know what time of the year it was, before I finally realized the cause of those agitated nights?

It is so difficult to believe that it has been two years since his last mortal words, "Gilda, I am fainting" resounded in my ears. It is two years since I felt his body relax in my arms and he was gone. What have I become in these two years? I know that my grieving and mourning days are gone, but my healing days continue. There are many days that I fervently wish for that closeness of touch, for the sweetness of waking in the morning to feel his body next to mine, for the two tired bodies clinging together as sleep overcomes in the night. Yes, I still desire this.

Even though his corporeal body is lost to me, I still sense his aura in the material things that are left. I can see and feel his clothing that hangs in the walk-in closet we shared. I wonder how much longer his blue bathrobe, hanging in the bathroom, will retain his scent; I notice that the odor is fading. His shirt still rides beside me in the car, and the most comforting thing of all is his voice on the answering machine.

As difficult as it is to believe, I have established a single life for myself. This life consists mostly of socializing with single women. Social interaction with couples is beyond my grasp. To a degree, I have become accepting of this separation from the coupled world. Is it because as a single person I am freer to make instant decisions, or is it that our times for socializing, day or night, are at odds with each other? Whatever the reason, our paths do not seem to cross.

My healing process is ongoing as I try to pursue a life for myself: a life composed of clinging to the past while working with the present.

Yes, I have arrived at a time, after two years, that when I finally come home at the end of a day, I am content to sit in the blue chair surrounded by the earthly effects of my beloved.

Now and then I wonder if I could accept a new male relationship, if the situation presented itself. Having the companionship of another would be comforting at times, but as yet, I don't believe that I am ready for this step.

I am content to be alone. I am ready to take on a new life in the evening of my years, and see what time brings to me, until Adonai, in His infinite wisdom, sends out another bolt of lightning!

This has been my journey. As it continues, my writing will allow me to communicate with my beloved, and his shirt, bathrobe and telephone answering machine voice will always ride with me.

Goals

Through these long and arduous months, I found that survival depended upon following certain essential goals. However, like anything else in life, goals are hard to attain—and if attained, to keep. As I think back in time, it took four attempts to stop smoking; finally, the fifth was a success. I cannot count the number of times I have tried to diet to control my weight. Each time was a dismal failure, until one day I found a diet that was in tune with my body, and I have had no trouble with weight since.

I have read many articles in health, mental health, and workout magazines. From these I have chosen the goals listed below to promote my mental and physical health. I admit that these goals are difficult; that is why they are goals. Some work on some days, and some rarely at all. But I have found that keeping them in mind and trying to achieve them, one day at a time, has made life more bearable.

- Keep my inner body healthy by eating regularly.

- Through yoga and walking, take care of my bones and my self-esteem.

- Keep my mind alert and help while away the hours between 4 and 6 p.m. by doing crossword puzzles and word games and reading.

- Try to keep my sense of humor.

- Above all, have a project to look forward to each day, a reason to get out of bed in the morning.

I wanted a perfect ending,
so I sat down to write the book
with the ending in place before
there even *was* an ending.
Now I've learned, the hard way,
that some poems don't rhyme,
and some stories don't have
a clear beginning, middle, and end.
Like my life, this book has ambiguity.
Like my life, this book is about
not knowing, having to change,
taking the moment and making the
best of it, without knowing
what's going to happen next.

—Gilda Radner, *It's Always Something*,
Simon & Schuster

Acknowledgements

I thought I could do it alone. I finally realized that it is very difficult to survive a period of mourning, and then days and months of grief, without people to support you.

In one way, I was very lucky in this chaotic period of my life. Somehow or other I managed to find people who were supportive during my most trying days. The two who helped me survive, and whom I blessed regularly, are my grief counselor, who let me sob and rant while she listened and occasionally asked leading questions that allowed me to delve deeper into my problems; and my daughter, who spent many afternoons with me reminiscing, talking, and crying about our loss.

Others helped me with the problem of my seemingly endless afternoons, when I felt lonely and abandoned and didn't know what to do with myself. It was during these long days that I developed a deeper friendship with three wonderful women I had known for many years. They were always available on those depressing afternoons, especially between three and four o'clock. These three women filled my deep need for companionship.

Through our conversations I realized that two of them, both widows, were undergoing or had undergone the same emotional upheavals that I experienced throughout that first year. One of the women, alone for many years, had found her own true course in life and was willing to impart her wisdom to me. The most remarkable development during this period of my life was that they were all willing to share with me, as I shared with them my mood swings and emotions. I realized that my problems were not a rarity but quite common, and were experienced by others as well. It was through this sharing and caring that the pain I felt on any individual day was eased, and I was able to return home feeling calmer. I was not really alone in this world.

Another person I must mention is my "telephone buddy." As soon as the Shiva period ended, my telephone started to ring at 9 a.m. every day and a familiar voice would say, "Good morning. I hope you have a very nice day," and hang up. This went on every day for about a year. As time went by, she inquired, "How do you feel?" or mentioned that my voice sounded sad or happy.

Now we have a system of check-in calls. There are times I call first to inquire, "How are you today?" or to state, "I hope you have a nice day," and hang up. We have established an essential part of living—awareness of someone else's welfare—through this buddy system. These check-in calls are not to be confused with times when we call each other for lunch dates or just plain talk. And we always notify the other if we will be out of town, so there is no concern when either of us does not pick up the phone. These calls are a very comforting way to start the day with a smile, and I am grateful for them.

My heartfelt thanks to the following people who have nurtured me, guided me, listened to me, stayed with me, and have not abandoned me on this journey:

Karen Zelin
Laura Davis
Melody Culver
Bobbie Bihn
Norma Caylin
Esther Wedner
Faye Alexander
Beverly Karp
Rabbi Paula Marcus

Glossary

Adonai—G-d.

Kaddish—a Jewish mourner's prayer that is central to the Jewish prayer service

phylacteries—(see *tefillin*)

seder—a special family meal filled with ritual that takes place during Passover and reminds participants of the significance of this holiday

Shiva—a period of five to seven days in which mourners stay at home, do no chores, and do not think about anything but the deceased. In some religious homes mirrors are covered, men do not shave, and the mourners sit on low stools and wear slippers

tallit—prayer shawl

tefillin—also called *phylacteries*, are two boxes containing Biblical verses and the leather straps attached to them which are used in traditional Jewish prayer

Talmud—a record of rabbinic discussions pertaining to Jewish law, ethics, customs and history

Unveiling—Ten to twelve months after the death of a beloved, a gravestone is erected and covered with a gauze material. On a predetermined date, the family, friends and a Rabbi gather. Certain prayers are said and the gauze is removed, unveiling the stone and inscription.

Yahrzeit—lighting a candle on the anniversary of the death of a mother, father, spouse or sibling. The date varies every year because the Jewish calendar has twenty-eight days to the month. To compensate for this, instead of a leap year (29 days in February), they have a leap month, using Adar I and Adar II. (Adar is one of the months in the Jewish calendar.)

978-0-595-46587-3
0-595-46587-0